A CHILDREN'S BOOK ABOUT COMPREHENSION, SELF-EXPLANATION, AND HOW TO MAKE SURE MAKE SURE YOU DON'T HAVE ANY BLIND SPOTS

FERDINAND LEARNS THE FEYNMAN TECHNIQUE

WRITTEN BY CHARLOTTE DANE, ILLUSTRATED BY MUTIARA ARUM

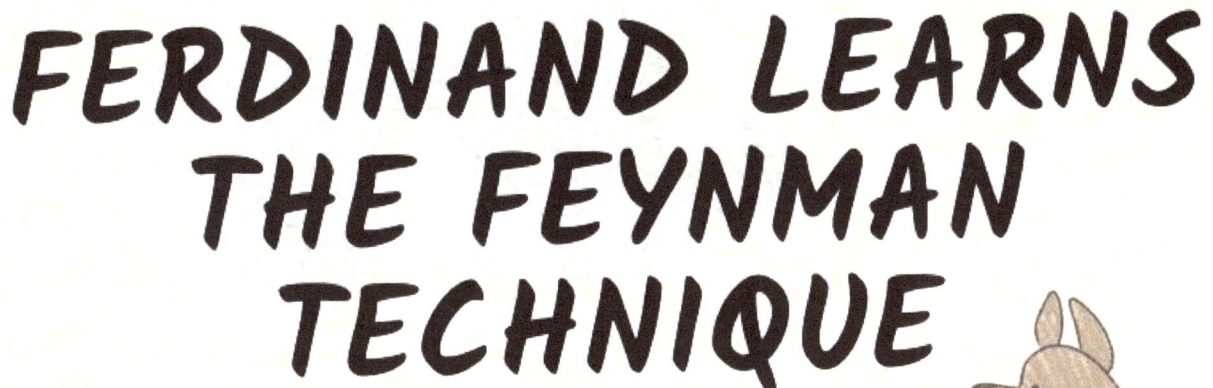

Learning is not easy. There's a reason we all need teachers, no matter how old we are.

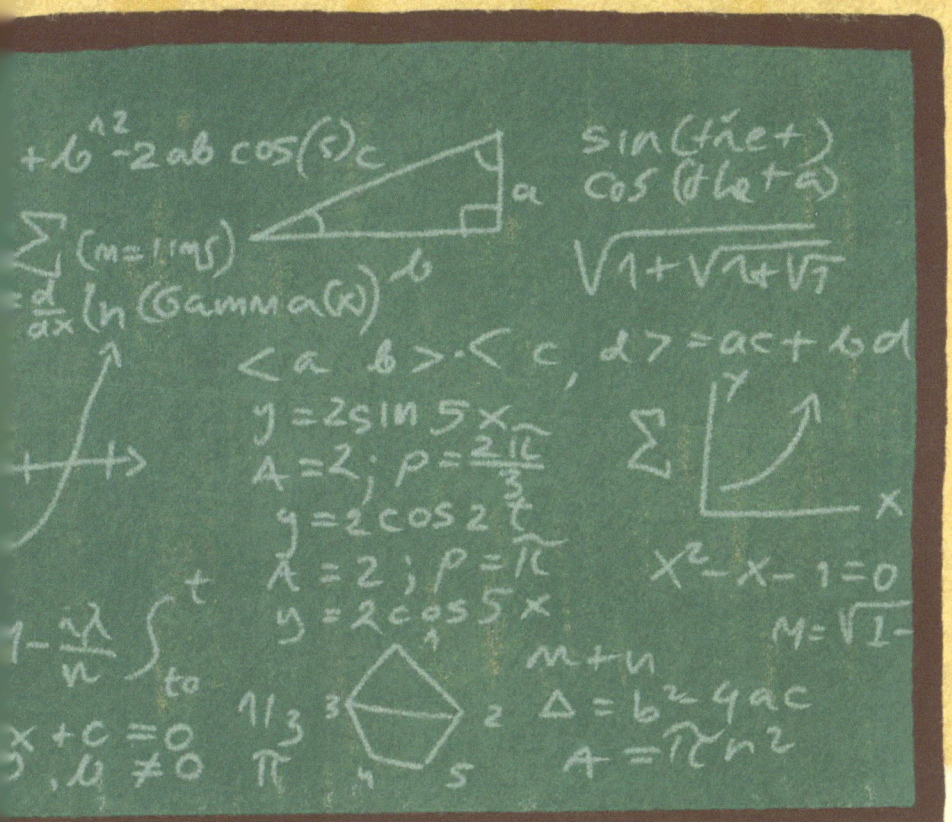

Sometimes we need to read something five times before we understand it! But Ferdinand had a pretty great method for understanding more quickly and efficiently.

For instance, when Ferdinand learned about the sun and the moon, he could explain the difference after 10 minutes, and even talked about the other planets.

His classmates were all in awe of him. He was so quick!

Ferdinand frequently understood things the fastest in his class. He had the most gold stars that year. He was so proud.

But Ferdinand wasn't always quick to absorb new material.

For example, two years ago, Ferdinand learned about Thomas Edison and how a light bulb works.

But when it came to the test, he couldn't explain how the light bulb worked and ended up just writing "magic". He failed that test.

Last year, he went on a road trip with his parents. It was going to be so fun, and he was responsible for looking at the directions.

He thought he understood it, but they got lost because he actually wasn't sure what some of the signs meant. He didn't make sure that he truly understood.

And more recently, Ferdinand tried using his credit card to buy a new tuxedo.

What was Ferdinand's issue?

Ferdinand would always rush and skip over things that he felt weren't important. He would just say "good enough, sort of like that" to himself and move on! Sometimes this was good enough, but sometimes this caused disaster! And his grades at school sure reflected it.

Ferdinand didn't really understand how tax and tip worked, so he paid far too much in tip! Freya saw what was going on.

She said, "Ferdinand, I think I see what's happening. You just don't spend much time trying to understand things."

"In fact, you try to do things so quickly that you get a lot wrong, and this time it cost you $10!"

"Let me teach you something that will help you to understand anything super quickly. It's called the Feynman Technique."

"There are 3 steps. First, you try to explain something out loud to yourself as simply as you can. It has to be a clear and complete explanation. Second, depending on how well you can do the first step, you can now see exactly where you have gaps in your knowledge. Third go fill those gaps until you can explain it 100% clearly and simply!"

Ferdinand was a little bit confused,
"But why should I explain it to myself?"

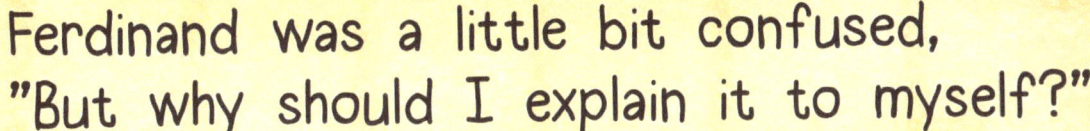

Freya said, "Because it forces you to test yourself. And when you test yourself, you can see exactly where you need help. You can see the small gaps that you can't get across yet. It's all about what you don't know, and that's what Feynman technique helps you with."

Ferdinand said, "But it's so easy! Watch: credit cards are when you use credit to buy things. Credit is... Oh, I see your point now." Ferdinand suddenly understood that he didn't know what he didn't understand.

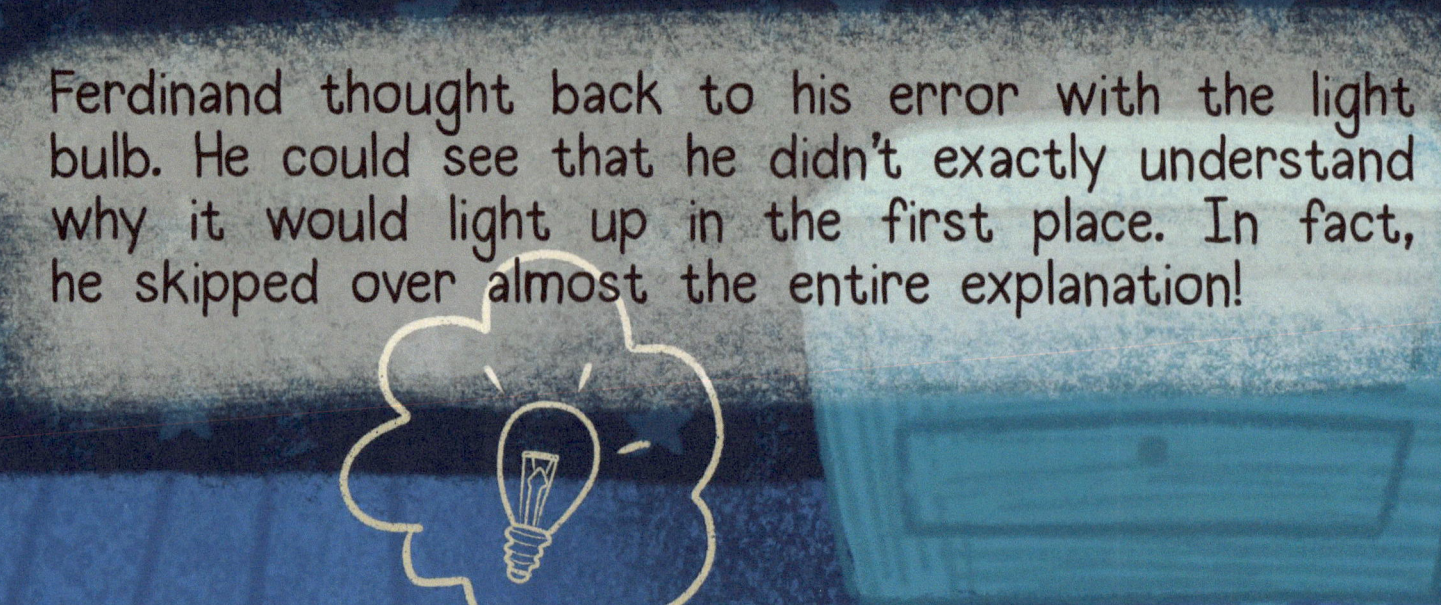

Ferdinand thought back to his error with the light bulb. He could see that he didn't exactly understand why it would light up in the first place. In fact, he skipped over almost the entire explanation!

So he went back to his textbook and made sure that he knew exactly why the light bulb works and how. What a huge difference!

And then Ferdinand tested himself on something new: why the sky is blue.

Instead of sticking with his first rushed explanation, he took his time until he could clearly explain to himself out loud what cause the blue coloring. He used the 3 steps of the Feynman Technique and kept trying until he filled all the gaps in his understanding.

Ferdinand was shocked. But as he continued to use the Feynman Technique, his grades got better and better

And the next time he took a road trip with his parents, he even found a shortcut that saved three hours!

Learning takes time and patience, but sometimes it just requires the right tool. The Feynman Technique is a tool that helps you figure out what you don't know.

It forces us to slow down and make sure that we are learning, not just reading, seeing, hearing, or repeating.

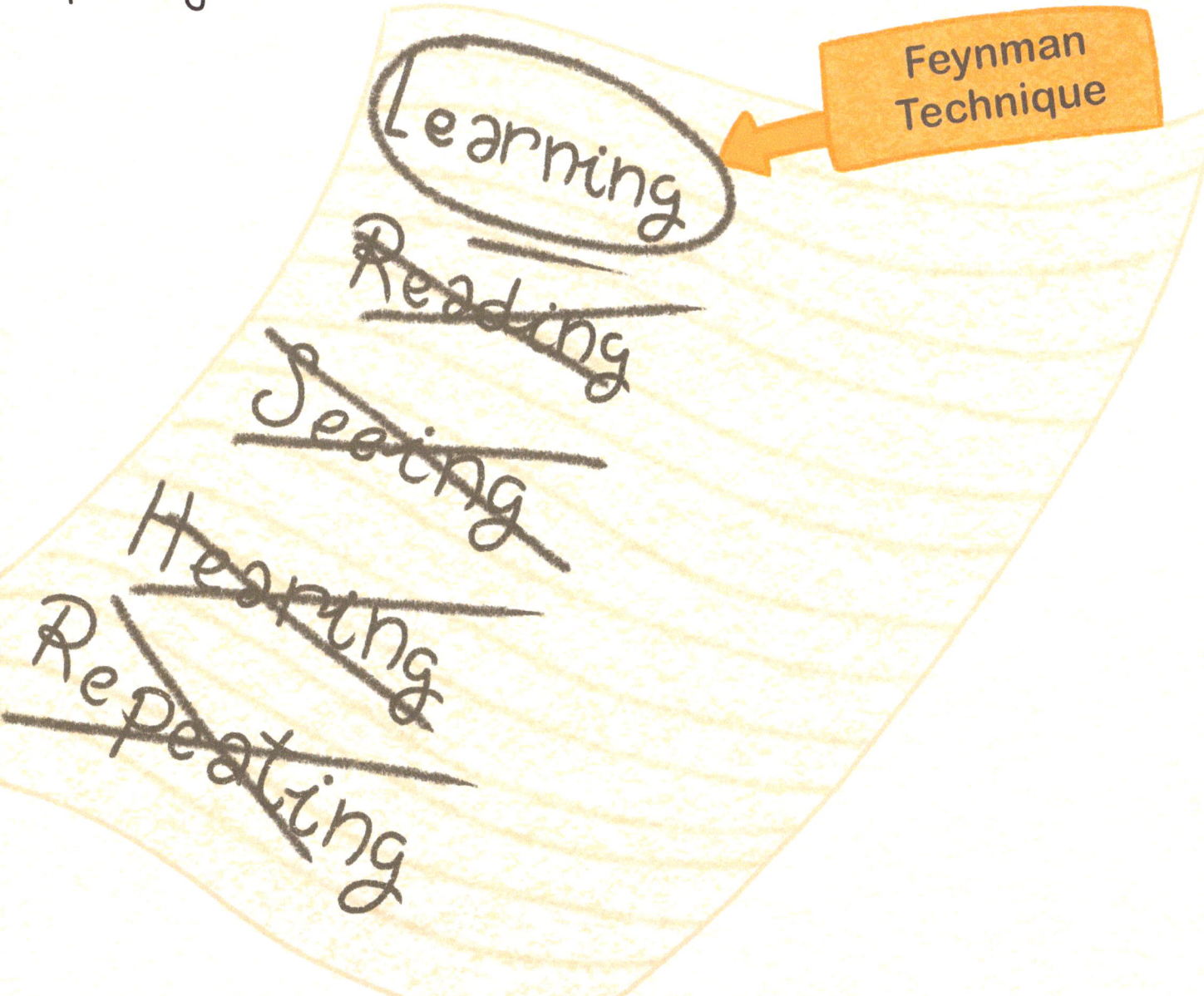

IN THIS BOOK, FERDINAND LEARNS ABOUT RICHARD FEYNMAN'S GREAT LEARNING TIP. HE AND HIS FRIEND FREYA LEARN ABOUT HOW TO MAKE SURE THAT THEY CAN LEARN NEW CONCEPTS AND IDEAS QUICKLY AND CLEARLY. MORE IMPORTANTLY, THEY WILL LEARN HOW TO DEFEAT THEIR BLIND SPOTS, THE THINGS THEY DIDN'T KNOW THAT THEY DIDN'T KNOW!

I'M LEARNING... IS A CHILDREN'S BOOK SERIES AIMED AT TEACHING CHILDREN ESSENTIAL LEARNING SKILLS, TO USE IN SCHOOL AND BEYOND. FOR MORE, VISIT BIGBARNPRESS.COM

In this book, Ferdinand learns about Richard Feynman's great learning tip. He and his friend Freya learn about how to make sure that they can learn new concepts and ideas quickly and clearly. More importantly, they will learn how to defeat their blind spots, the things they didn't know that they didn't know!

I'm Learning... is a children's book series aimed at teaching children essential learning skills, to use in school and beyond. For more, visit bigbarnpress.com

www.ingramcontent.com/pod-product-compliance
Lightning Source LLC
Chambersburg PA
CBHW041455220226
40083CB00017B/893